MW00587647

WHY CHILDREN MATTER

WHY
CHILDREN
MATTER

DOUGLAS WILSON

canonpress
Moscow, Idaho

Published by Canon Press
P.O. Box 8729, Moscow, Idaho 83843
800.488.2034 | www.canonpress.com
Printed in the United States of America.

Douglas Wilson, *Why Children Matter*
Copyright ©2018 by Douglas Wilson. The appendix is selected and edited from several Q&A sessions with Doug and Nancy Wilson.

Cover illustration by Forrest Dickison. Cover design by James Engerbretson. Interior layout by Valerie Anne Bost.

Unless otherwise indicated, all Scripture quotations are from the King James Version. Those marked "NKJV" are from the New King James Version®. Copyright ©1982 by Thomas Nelson, Inc., and those marked "ESV" are from the ESV® Bible (The Holy Bible, English Standard Version®), copyright © 2001 by Crossway, a publishing ministry of Good News Publishers. Used by permission. All rights reserved.

All rights reserved. No part of this publication may be reproduced, stored in a retrieval system, or transmitted in any form by any means, electronic, mechanical, photocopy, recording, or otherwise, without prior permission of the author, except as provided by USA copyright law.

Library of Congress Cataloging-in-Publication Data:
Wilson, Douglas, 1953- author.
Why children matter / Douglas Wilson.
Moscow : Canon Press, 2018.
LCCN 2018024494 | ISBN 1947644424 (pbk. : alk. paper)
LCSH: Child rearing—Religious aspects—Christianity. |
 Parenting—Religious aspects—Christianity.
Classification: LCC BV4529 .W5855 2018 | DDC 248.8/45--dc23
LC record available at https://lccn.loc.gov/2018024494

18 19 20 21 22 23 21 22 23   10 9 8 7 6 5 4 3 2

This is for Moses,
who is part of the reason
why grandchildren matter also.

CONTENTS

PART ONE: WHY CHILDREN MATTER

PART TWO: DISCIPLINE BASICS

PART THREE:
NURTURE AND ADMONITION

PART FOUR: MORE LIKE CHRIST

PART ONE

WHY
CHILDREN
MATTER

CHAPTER 1

THE DEFINITION OF FAMILY

The family is a divinely ordained community. The institution of the family—consisting of one man, one woman, and their children—was created by God, not by people. It is not an arbitrary collection of individuals, and it is not something that mere creatures get to define.

Congress can no more vote on what the family is than they can vote on whether gravity exists or not. It is possible Congress could decree that water flow uphill, but no matter how hard they vote, they cannot change what God has previously done. Similarly, if Congress voted to repeal the law of gravity, and some people decided to jump off a cliff or a skyscraper, the people jumping might have a sensation of liberty for a moment—*we're flying!*—but nothing would change the reality of what gravity is and does. In the same way, even if the Supreme Court outlawed marriage, while it could destroy a lot of people's lives, it would not destroy the reality of marriage itself. Marriage was established by God at the very beginning of the world. It is not going anywhere any time soon.

Since the family was not invented by us in the first place, we do not get to *re*invent it. For this reason, parents must beware of treating the family as something cobbled together and managed with techniques developed by experts. So you should not begin this small book by thinking that it is a collection of clever techniques for getting the perfect family. Each person in the family is a being made in the image of God, and if we are to manage the family properly, we must heed God's Word as our first and most important guide. That includes treating all the people in the family as though they were *people*, not place-holding counters.

When someone talks about family or child-drearing or other practical matters, it is easy for Americans to start wishing for books with titles like *Three Steps to . . .* or *Twelve Steps to . . .* or *Secrets of . . .* etc. But this book is not an exercise in therapeutic self-help—it is nothing less than a proclamation of the gospel as embodied in family life. If you are looking at your family and you are not seeing gospel principles, then you are looking at your family with your eyes shut.

Young parents in particular should come to the Scriptures with a hunger for instruction on how to perform this task, especially those who did not have a good example from their own parents. Parents can give their children something that their own parents did not give them, because our God breaks cycles of sin. Even if you did not have a great parental model for being a godly father or mother, you are not limited to imitating people who are right there next to you. Learning by imitation is a great blessing and help, but the Bible teaches us that we can imitate others from what has been written down as well, whether from biographies or from examples in Scripture itself. God is the God of new beginnings, and He blesses to a thousand generations. When God says He visits iniquity to three and four generations, that is not a dire threat, but an act of mercy. This is because God is *limiting* the cascading effects of sin.

The title of this small book is *Why Children Matter*, but I should probably expand it to *Why Children Matter to All of Us*. The gospel principles described here have application everywhere, but particularly in the family when you are bringing up children. Moreover, if you are reading this and think you have nothing to do with children, I would encourage you to pay close attention anyway: when I was single and in the Navy, home ported out of Norfolk, I attended Tabernacle Church. It was a great church, and they had a thriving Christian school associated with it. If I had known that within a few years I would be in the midst of trying to start a Christian school, I would have paid much closer attention to what was going on in that school, because it turned out, there was a lot for me to learn. Even if you are a very young man and still trying to figure out her father's phone number, you should pay attention. As a

matter of fact, if you are trying to get her father's number, you are far down the road we
are talking about.

CHAPTER 2

BE MIMICS OF GOD

Therefore be imitators of God, as beloved children.
EPHESIANS 5:1 ESV

E phesians 5:1 says that we are to be imitators of God. I chose the English Standard Version here because the King James Version has "be *followers* of God," but the Greek word for "followers" is actually where we get the words "mimesis" and "mimetic." Paul is telling us to mimic, to *copy*, God. We are God's beloved children, and we are to look to Him as children look to their father.

God has created us to be reflective and imitative creatures. We imitate instinctively and naturally. Not only do we imitate those who are shoulder-to-shoulder with us, such as our friends, colleagues, co-workers, and family members, but we also pick up many things from those above us. We learn how to walk and talk from our parents, but the fundamental imitation the Bible calls us to is imitation of the One we worship.

Idolaters become like what they worship. Psalm 115:4–8 says that the idolaters worship statues that have eyes that do not see, ears that do not hear, noses that do not smell, and then caps it all off by saying that "they that make them are like unto them." If you worship something that is deaf, dumb, and blind, then you are going to become deaf, dumb, and blind yourself. If your god is stone cold, you are going to become stone cold. If your god is ultimately impersonal, this will result in you becoming less and less personlike.

Worshipers of the true God also become like what they worship, as Paul points out in 2 Corinthians 3:18: "But we all, with open face beholding as in a glass the glory of the Lord, are changed into the same image from glory to glory, even as by the Spirit of the Lord." The God we worship is the sun that shines on us; we are the moon and we reflect Him. As we face God in worship, we are being transformed from one degree of glory to another, and as we are transformed, we too wish to pass that glory on to our children.

There are few places where the ramifications of this principle of imitation are as important as in childrearing. Imitation is absolutely crucial for childrearing. You do not want your children imitating you unless you are imitating God. If you are not imitating and pursuing God, sincerely and openly beholding His face in worship weekly, being transformed from one degree of glory to another, then the last thing you should want is for your children to imitate you. However, the bad news is that your children will copy you regardless of whether you want them to or not. When your child is born, you might cast around for an instruction manual. You may feel as if you have no idea what you are doing. However, there is a false premise in the worry—you *do* have a Bible. You must worship God, imitate Him, and ask Him to walk with you as you take up the challenge of being a parent.

We tend to think that might is used destructively, in order to impose on someone else. But how does God use His might? His might is employed for the good of His people and for their salvation and maturity. God wants His people to be saved, and the might of His arm is what He uses to save us. He wants us to grow up. He does not want to smother us or suffocate us with a relationship that we cannot get out of. He does not *make* us become like Him; He invites us to grow up in imitation of Him, and His Spirit helps us as we grow.

Sometimes when grown children go home for Thanksgiving, their parents ask them why they do not come home more often. In these cases, it might be because parents are demanding and clingy. Ironically, when parents bring up their children with a godly, biblical independence in view, their children actually want to spend time with them when they are grown up.

Your purpose as parents is ultimately to be the instrument of your children's salvation. You are not the ground of their salvation, but you are commanded to imitate the One who is the ground of their salvation. It is the same with marriage. Husbands cannot offer themselves as a vicarious, substitutionary atonement for their wives. The only One who can do that is Jesus. However, husbands are commanded to *imitate* that which they *cannot* do. It is the same with parents. Parents, you are not able to save your children. You cannot just press a button or make a decision and be the ground of your children's salvation. You obviously cannot be their saving grace, but you are commanded to imitate that saving grace and to facilitate it and have it permeate the atmosphere of your home. God is mighty and able to save.

CHAPTER 3

SACRIFICE WITH SINGING

The Lord thy God in the midst of thee is mighty; he will save, he will rejoice over thee with joy; he will rest in his love, he will joy over thee with singing.

ZEPHANIAH 3:17

L et's now consider this verse from Zephaniah and place it in juxtaposition to Ephesians 5:1. Ephesians says that God treats us as children. Since Scripture shows how He treats us, we should desire to be like

Him in how we treat *our* children. As He deals with us, so we should deal with our own children. And we see from Zephaniah that He rejoices over us.

When Jesus intervened to save us, He did so at great cost to Himself. When He took the loaf of bread that represented His own broken body, He picked it up *and gave thanks*. As Hebrews 12 says, Jesus did what He did on the cross "for the joy that was set before Him." Our sacred meal is called the Eucharist. What does that mean? *Eucharisto* is the Greek word for thanksgiving, which means that a Eucharistic meal is a thanksgiving meal. It *is* a thanksgiving meal, not only because we thank God for what Jesus did for us, but also because He thanked God when He instituted it. That is the kind of rejoicing spirit that we see in Zephaniah. God is mighty to save, and He saves with singing.

Now we know from the story of the whole Bible that saving people involves sacrifice, blood, and things being broken. He who knew no sin was made to be sin for us, but He did it with singing. Not only did Jesus give thanks the night He instituted the meal, but afterward they sang a psalm, and then they went out (Matt. 26:30;

Mark 14:26). Jesus literally *sang* as He was preparing to go to the cross.

So, the sacrifices that you will make for your children should be something you can sing over. If there is not a song in it, it is not a biblical sacrifice. Without a song, it is a poor-me, look-at-the-martyr-go sacrifice, and *those* kinds of sacrifices have a very poor return. You are not just supposed to sing over your children when they are being adorable, asleep in their bed, and you can be at peace with them since they are not misbehaving at the moment. Life is messier than that, and the whole thing—including the mess—should be met with a song. The delight that we are imitating is not an unrealistic delight. This kind of delight takes account of the world as it is, and even so, it rejoices. You sing over your children when you are sacrificing for them, when you are taking the hit for them, and when they have no idea what you are giving up for them.

You even need to rejoice when they want to leave home and do their own thing, whether that involves joining the Navy or going away to college. Hopefully, as a parent, you actually are preparing for them to grow up—and not just to keep having nice conversations with Mom. "Therefore shall a man leave his father and his mother, and shall cleave unto his wife: and they shall be one flesh" (Gen. 2:24). Sons leave, daughters are given. There are many sentimental, conservative, and evangelical parents who are at war with this and want to put that day off. When parents chafe because their children have jobs or spouses and children which prevent them from spending time with them, they are struggling against the way God designed the world.

Of course, I am not saying that you should *avoid* a relationship with your grown kids and your grandkids. Psalm 103:17 says that "the mercy of the Lord is from everlasting to everlasting upon them that fear him, and his righteousness *unto children's children.*" We are to rejoice over our children's children. We are to be involved, not as a suffocating blanket, but rejoicing over everything new that God is giving to them.

CHAPTER 4

ONE NO IN
A WORLD OF YES

W hen God first created the human
race, He placed Adam in a garden
full of delights, with just one prohibition in the middle of that garden. Outside the
garden, *nothing* was prohibited, and inside the
garden, only *one* thing was prohibited. Further, I
believe that the tree of the knowledge of good and
evil was meant to be prohibited only for a time,
and after they passed their prohibitory test, God
was going to let them eat from that tree. When
Adam and Eve grabbed the fruit of the tree, they

were judged for grabbing *prematurely*, not because the knowledge of good and evil was a bad thing in itself. Throughout Scripture, knowledge of good and evil is what kings use as they rule (e.g., 1 Kings 3:9). This is the kind of knowledge that helps kings judge rightly. But Adam and Eve were not yet prepared for that.

But regardless of whether that prohibition was going to be lifted down the road or not, even though Adam and Eve disobeyed that one prohibition and were punished as a result, God saw to it that the severest blow of retaliation for that sin fell upon Himself. What kind of God is this? God gave Adam a perfect world, a perfect wife, a perfect environment, a perfect commission, a perfect vocation, and then, even when Adam and Eve transgressed, doing the one thing in that perfect world that was not permitted, even then God promised that the seed of the woman would destroy the seed of the serpent, crushing its head (Gen. 3:15).

Imitate *that*. The environment of your home should be full of grace. When you have a home filled with grace, it is not without standards. You are not introducing moral anarchy. Grace is not an amorphous, gelatinous mass. Grace has a backbone. However, when the standards are broken, the heaviest sacrifices in the work of restoration are made by the guardians of grace, not by enforcers of law, finger-pointers, parental accusers, or people who correct in a nasal tone of self-pity.

Imagine your kids have disobeyed, and as a result you say to them, "How do you think it makes *me* feel when you do that? I've told you five thousand times not to do that." While it is true that repetition is a necessary part of childrearing, the quaver of self-pity and exasperation in the voice is not. That is not a biblical way of shepherding young people, because young people learn by imitation. When you see an adult feeling sorry for himself, your immediate response is not to say, "Oh, you poor baby." When you're full of self-pity, your kids *are* learning a lesson. But what they learn is not to feel sorry for *you*, but rather how to say, "How do you think that makes *me* feel?" It turns out that more than one person can say that.

If you model selfishness, you are going to get selfishness. It is the easiest thing in the world to find a moral standard in the Bible and then to be selfish with it. If you are a parent being selfish, you are modeling selfishness. A garden of grace can contain a tree of law. A garden of law cannot contain a tree of grace. If your garden is all law, and there is a tree of grace in the middle of it, it is not really grace. It is a tree of merit, and you are going to have kids that are just good for the sake of the reward: "I was good, can I have my treat now?"

I know that to say the atmosphere in your home must be "all grace" may seem to be gibberish, or a sort of Zen Presbyterianism, but bear with me for a moment. Mark Twain was a profane man, and he often used a lot of bad language, and his wife did not like it at all. One day she decided to let him have it, and so she went up to him and calmly recited to him every word that she had heard him say. He looked at her and then said, "My dear, you know the words, but you don't know the tune." Now, flip that around: many Christians know the words "grace," "tender mercies," and "forgiveness," *but they don't know the tune*. Our tune can be found in the passage from the previous chapter: Zephaniah 3:17. God *rejoices* over us with singing.

When discipline is directed toward an end, it has a purpose. No discipline seems pleasant at the time, but the glory of discipline is found in the harvest (Heb. 12:11). Bringing your children up is not abstract bookkeeping, but rather a story that spans from plowing and planting to harvest. It is a story, and you need to have your eye on the story so that when you discipline your children it is with an eye on the harvest—in this case, for the sake of their own good. The harvest comes when they too realize the peaceful fruit of an upright life.

When you are an adult, you are the one who has grown up and who understands time. When you are a three-year-old, one year is a third of your entire existence. As a parent, it is just another telephone pole by the highway, and thus you parents should have a better grasp of time and story than your toddlers . . . right?

Hardship in a story is grace; hardship without a story is just pain. Childrearing is the opportunity that you have to love your children in preparation for a harvest, but that means you need to have the harvest in mind.

CHAPTER 5

THE THREE L's

W hen it comes to Christian living, there are three L's to choose from: legalism, license, and liberty. In the home, legalism occurs when parents try to establish traditional values or a disciplined atmosphere on their own authority for their own sake. They want the kids to behave so that it is not an irritant to them. They tell their kids not to careen around the living room because it bothers them and gets on their nerves. Instead, they should do it because they want their children to learn self-control, so they will be prepared when they go out into the world as adults. We should correct children for *their* sakes, not for our own.

With legalism, strictness becomes the central standard. License happens when parents realize that legalism involves a lot of work. It turns out that when you pester people all the time, then they rebel against you, and it blows up in your face. As a result, parents just abandon all standards, rejecting it all as a bunch of legalistic foolishness, and soon their parenting is nothing more than a long stream of excuses and lame theories on the ineffectiveness of spanking that they circulate on Facebook. If you have told twenty-eight people this week that "he missed his nap today" as an excuse for his disobedience, then perhaps you ought to re-evaluate. We all know there are times when this is not an excuse but a reasonable explanation. But if you find yourself resorting to excuses all the time, then you are just trying to get people to overlook your lack of wisdom and discipline.

Liberty is not a middle position between legalism and license; it is another thing entirely. We have a hard time with this. Liberty is not moderate legalism or moderated license. *Liberty is stricter than legalism, and liberty is freer than license.* Jesus tells His disciples, "Except your righteousness shall exceed the righteousness of the scribes and Pharisees, ye shall in no case enter into the kingdom of heaven" (Matt. 5:20). He is not telling them to be moderate Pharisees but to surpass the Pharisees.

Liberty was purchased for us by Christ on the cross, not by our shifts and evasions. The righteousness of liberty outdoes the legalist, and the joy of liberty outdoes the libertine. If you want to be a godly Christian parent without being a godly Christian who dies to yourself and your desires, then you have got everything all wrong from the beginning. Grace is what we must all learn as individual Christians, learning to worship God sincerely as both individuals and as godly fathers and mothers. Living with an environment of grace that encompasses law is something that only the Spirit of God can give you. If you sing over your children as you delight in imitating God, your children will pick up on it. That's how the world works.

So where we are going? Children are creatures bearing the image of God. As sinners, that image is defaced in them because they are affected by Adam's sin just like the rest of us, but as saints that image is being restored in them as it is in us. They are fallen as we are fallen, but the image of Jesus Christ is being established in them just as it is in us.

Now that Christ has come and redeemed us from the curse of the law, we are given the opportunity, as Paul says, to bring up our children "in the nurture and admonition of the Lord" (Eph. 6:4). Children are included in the book of Ephesians in the sixth chapter, but it is still part of the same process that Paul began describing in chapter 1. God's purposes and the good counsel of His will include our children, and therefore raising them up in the fear and admonition of the Lord means that both you and they are putting off the old man and putting on the new. You and your children are putting off the old man. You and your children are putting on the new man. God is after a lineage, and He's been after a lineage from the very beginning. Why did God make them one? He was seeking a "godly seed" (Mal. 2:15).

That's why children matter.

PART TWO

DISCIPLINE BASICS

CHAPTER 6

CHILDREN OF GOD

Thou shalt also consider in thine heart,
that, as a man chasteneth his son,
so the Lord thy God chasteneth thee.
DEUTERONOMY 8:5, KJV

I have written many times that theology comes out your fingertips. Regardless of what you say you believe, your theology of justification and sanctification is enacted in microcosm in your relationship to your children. That may make you scratch your head for a moment, but remember that we not only want to learn how to discipline our children in a biblical fashion, but that we also want to do so in a biblical context. So this small book is not a set of techniques, and the Scriptures are not a quarry from which we gather our self-help rocks. We only want one rock: the cornerstone, our Lord Jesus Christ.

We are bringing up our children as Christians are called to do, and you cannot bring up Christian children as Christians outside the context of the gospel. We are seeking to understand everything we are doing in the context of gospel grace. This is not a set of techniques for moral, decent, respectable, middle-class people. We are pursuing the subject as Christians who have been delivered by the gospel of Jesus Christ, and we want to be used by God in leading our children in that same deliverance.

Deuteronomy 8:5 explicitly says that the Lord has a relationship with us that is mirrored in the relationship that a father has with his son. This is a truth that needs to be *considered*, and not just acknowledged. Moses tells the people to consider in your heart and meditate on this: a man chastens his son, and God does the same thing for His children.

When we are saved, God adopts us into His family, and that means that we are in a parent-child relationship with God. The Lord Jesus teaches us to pray, "Our *Father*, who art in heaven." Jesus says, "I am the way, the truth, and the life: no man cometh unto the *Father*, but by me" (John 14:6). So God is our Father. The Scriptures often distinguish between justification and sanctification. Justification establishes the *fact* of this relationship, while sanctification determines the *direction* of the relationship. The fact of this relationship is that you are a child of God by the free gift of God's grace. Sanctification is the process of God communicating to us what He wants us to be as we grow up in His family. God does not spank the neighbors' children: He spanks His own. The pains of sanctification bear witness to the fact that we are His children. There is no such thing as sanctification without direction, and direction means discipline.

We look at what the Bible says about God the Father and us in order to learn how we should discipline our children. We also look at how we discipline our children and learn things about our relationship with God. The way we treat our children is not always a good way to learn about God, but sometimes by God's grace we do the right thing, and it provides us an opportunity to learn more about what God is doing in our own lives.

CHAPTER 7

FOUR PRINCIPLES FOR DISCIPLINE

D iscipline, rightly considered, is a form of wisdom. If it is not, then it cannot impart wisdom. Discipline is painful, but not everything that is painful is discipline. We have to be adults in our thinking—dogs have four legs but not everything with four legs is a dog. So let us consider some principles for discipline, each of which is reflected in God's relationship with us.

First, discipline is *not* punishment. Discipline has correction in view, while punishment has justice and retribution in view. Capital punishment, for instance, does not have the correction of the criminal in mind. It might happen in the goodness and kindness of God that someone who is on death row cries out to God and gets converted, but that is not the point of capital punishment. One of the great errors of our day is that we have tried to have the civil magistrate take over the job of discipline. Why do we have penitentiaries? That is where you go to become penitent. The whole system of the penitentiary was built by the state to do the familial work of discipline, which the civil magistrate is not competent to do. The civil magistrate is assigned the sword (Rom. 13), not the spanking spoon.

The Bible teaches us that parents are to discipline their children, not to punish them. Hebrews 12:11 says, "now no chastening for the present seemeth to be joyous but grievous: nevertheless afterward it yieldeth the peaceable fruit of righteousness unto them which are exercised thereby." Discipline has harvest or objective in view, either because we have a problem that we have to correct (the negative form of discipline) or we have immaturity or weakness that has to be built up (the positive form of discipline). However, discipline always wants to go from here to there to accomplish something.

You do not put each of your kids in the bathtub for an equal length of time in the interests of fairness. Some kids need to be in the tub for shorter amounts of time, and some need to be in it longer because they have dirt all the way down to their brain. Spanking and disciplining your children and correcting attitudes is disciplinary, not punitive, and the whole point of it is so that you can get to a certain place. You should not think of yourself as a magistrate or as a judge meting out justice from on high. Both discipline and punishment are good in their place, but they are not the same thing. Parents (particularly with small children) ought not to be thinking in terms of judgment or retribution at all.

Second, make sure that you discipline not with many rules but rather with a few *principles*. You are a parent, not a regulatory agency. Specific applications can always be deduced from the principles, but you cannot achieve the same result by inducing the principles from a host of particular commands. I remember when

I was a child, my father delivered three rules to me. Not only that, but I also remember where I was standing in the front yard when he delivered them to me, and I remember the fond and affectionate demeanor with which he delivered it (he had his fist in front of my face). His three principles were *1) No disobedience, 2) No lying,* and *3) No disrespecting your mother.* Now, what is not covered by that?

Focus on the root laws, and not on the leaves on the ends of the twigs. Jesus teaches that there are two great commandments that summarize the whole Old Testament: love the Lord your God with all your heart and love your neighbor as yourself (Matt. 22:37–40). These two commands correspond to the Ten Commandments—the greatest commandment corresponds to the first four commandments, and the next greatest corresponds to the last six. All the other laws in the Old Testament can fit under either of those commands. Discipline by principle means that your system of discipline makes sense. It is orderly. It is not a chaos of commandments that depend upon the emotional state of Mom or Dad at the time the directives are delivered.

One of the reasons people multiply commandments is if they want to catch somebody, they
always have something to catch them on. (I have
no doubt that the vast majority of you are disobeying some governmental regulation as you
sit reading this book.) But that is the way ty-
rants think, not the way parents ought to think.
You ought to think in terms of "keep it simple,
keep it straightforward." God has given us the
Bible, and you can reduce the Old Testament
law to ten requirements that can fit on an in-
dex card—and after that you can reduce it again
down to two.

But if we said "What does the United States
Congress want us to do?" we would have to fill
up shelf after shelf after shelf of regulations.
This is because the federal government is not
after obedience, but rather is trying to control
your life. Parents must not be that way.

Remember that God gave Adam and Eve a
perfect garden: there was a world full of yes,
and there was only one no. Minimize the number of no's in your home. This is another way of
saying that you should pick your battles careful-
ly as parents. Suppose that over the space of a
month, you have issued a hundred commands,

and the kids have been constantly disobeying them. It would be far better for you to reduce those hundred commands to ten commands, and enforce every one of those ten, than to keep it at a hundred and enforce a fifth of the time. The parent with a hundred commands may get compliance on more occasions than the other, but the batting average is terrible. And you in- still confusion by having your child never know when Dad is going to come down on you, or when Mom is going to flare up. Their world is going to be far more stable and secure if you *reduce* the number of requirements you place on them, but insist on obedience every time. It's all a matter of percentages.

Third, keep calm. Correction is needed when somebody has messed up, but the Bible tells us how the correction is to be brought: "Brethren, if a man be overtaken in a fault, ye which are spiri- tual, restore such an one in a spirit of meekness; considering thyself, lest thou also be tempted" (Gal. 6:1). This passage tells us how we ought to correct one another in the Body. When we baptize children, one of the things the parents promise to do is to treat that child as a brother or sister in the Lord.

When you are highly motivated to discipline your children, you are, according to this passage, *not qualified to do so*. And by "highly motivated," I don't mean motivated by the Holy Spirit, but motivated by your nerves, your anger, or your passion. You have one nerve, and your kids are on it, so you flare up and then crack down. However, you are cracking down because of your emotional zeal to get them to *shut up*. You are not disciplining them because they have transgressed the Word of God, but because your pride was affronted.

Galatians 6:1 says that if you go to correct a brother, you must be spiritual: "Restore such an one in a spirit of meekness; considering thyself lest thou also be tempted." Whenever you are disciplining your children, you are being tempted. You have to go into it considering *yourself*, lest you be tempted and fall. But, when you are qualified to discipline, you do not always feel motivated to do it. Suppose you are at peace with God and the world, there in your La-Z-boy watching the game, and one of your kids disregards something their mother said. You may be qualified to discipline at this point, but because you are, you do not feel like it. But even if you do not feel like it, your discipline needs to be principled and based on what God wants you to do in that moment, and not based on your emotional state. Your emotional state might feel like disciplining when you should not, or it might feel like not disciplining when you should, so you cannot base discipline on the state of your emotions. In order to teach obedience, your disciplining must be *itself* obedient and disciplined.

I mentioned the phrase "qualified to discipline." Do not make the mistake of thinking that you are not qualified to discipline your children if you were guilty of the same sin when you were a kid. Your requirement to discipline has to be based on what God tells you to do in this moment, not based on whether you were the kind of kid you ought to have been. If you were not the kind of kid you ought to have been, then you don't fix that by refusing to be the kind of parent you ought to be. You ought to repent and start doing it God's way now. Qualifications to discipline are present or not in the moment of discipline.

True discipline is about restored fellowship. When sin occurs, it disrupts fellowship in the family. Discipline seeks to address that disruption in order to undo the effects (Eph. 4:32). There are different ways that this can go wrong. If there is no fellowship to begin with, it is impossible to restore it. If your kid's life is chronic pain all the time thanks to your carping and their disobedience, with periodic moments of acute pain which you call "discipline," their response to discipline will be something like, "I hate you, I hate you, I hate you." A child who does not want to go back into the garden of fellowship is likely living outside the garden *all the time*.

If the moments of discipline just drive your children farther away, that should reveal something to you. Maybe they were never in the garden of fellowship in the first place, and maybe you need to do something about *that*. But if they are in fellowship with you, and your home is a happy home, then when sin disrupts it and you discipline them, they will want back in. That is a healthy sign.

The other way this can go wrong is if discipline is meted out in anger. Godly discipline subtracts from the number of offenses; it does not add to them. If a child is disobedient and there are two or three things that have disrupted the fellowship in the home, and if you discipline in anger, the home's fellowship is more disrupted than ever. The "discipline" did not help. If the disciplinary moment adds to the offenses, it is not discipline. Discipline subtracts, restores, and puts you back to where you ought to be. If discipline is not doing that, you probably do not have loving, Christian fellowship in the home at all.

I'd like to add one more thing to this third principle for discipline: keep calm *and spank anyway*. I said earlier that in Galatians 6:1, you are commanded to correct your brother, considering yourself lest you also be tempted. Even then, you do this the way God says to do it. The discipline of spanking is not to be understood as a form of self-expression. It is a form of correction, and it is a way of pleasing God. It is not a way to vent your feelings. If you need to spank in order to vent your feelings, you are not qualified. Spanking needs to be far more judicial and calm than that. However, if you stay calm, and you are motivated by obedience to the Word of God, what does God say? In Proverbs 23:13–14 it says, "Withhold not correction from the child: for if thou beatest him with a rod, he shall not die. Thou shalt beat him with the rod, and shalt deliver his soul from hell." In this we are imitating our Father: Hebrews 12:6 tells us that God scourges every son that He receives.

We live in a time when a number of very foolish Christian parents have attempted to discipline foolishly, found out that *that* does not work, and concluded that the problem must be with God's Word, and not with their own inept applications of it. If it was a sinful spanking, you ought not to do it that way, rather than refusing to deal with it at all. God's Word tells us what we are to do. Do not reject what the Bible plainly teaches. If you refuse, then you are failing to head your child off as he is headed for destruction.

Yes, corporal discipline is taught in the Bible, but that does not mean that you have to spank your kids every ten minutes whether they need it or not. We are not talking about child abuse— spankings should sting, but never damage.

"Spanking fails" happen in two ways: one is when you clobber a kid, and he learns to stay away every time you stub your toe or turn on the television. That is simply abuse. Slugging your kids is not what God calls you to, and if that is something you do, you must repent and seek forgiveness from God and from your children. You are never permitted to beat your kids up.

The other kind of fail, and frankly the far more common one, is when you deliver the occasional and very inconsistent *wumph* on top of the diapers. What happens is you just moved your kid six inches, and that is the only thing that happened. Your demon-child responds to this by saying to herself, "Ha! I defy you and all your pitiful attempts at intimidating the queen of the world!"

Discipline is a universal language. It communicates. Godly discipline gets through. If it does not get the attention, it is not godly discipline. Many times, parents are reluctant to discipline when it is needed, because they think their child is feeble-minded when it comes to godly cause and effect. A mom says, "I don't think my little baa-lamb"—known to outsiders as the wailing tornado, and to his siblings as Rasputin in footie jammies—"understands the connection between the whining and the spanking. He looks so sad and bewildered." Doesn't understand disciplinary cause and effect, you say?

But how can this be, when he is a veritable genius when it comes to *ungodly* cause and effect? Tell me, does he understand the connection between whining and getting whatever it is he wants? He understands *those* causal relationships . . . so why can he not understand the causal relationship between flipping out and discipline? In Proverbs 19:19 it says, "A man of great wrath shall suffer punishment: for if thou deliver him, yet thou must do it again." This is the principle of cause and effect. If someone loses his temper, and you clean up after him, regardless of whether he is a two-year-old, a thirty-year-old, or a sixty-year-old, you are going to have to do it again. You are *paying* your child to be that way. You get more of what you subsidize and less of what you penalize.

Fourth, discipline is love. The Bible states this both ways: first, it says it positively. "For whom the Lord loveth, he chasteneth" (Hebrews 12:6). If God loves you, he chastens you. The same principle is stated negatively just a moment later: "But if ye be without chastisement, whereof all are partakers, then are ye bastards, and not sons" (Heb. 12:8). In Proverbs 13:24, we have the principle stated negatively: "He that spareth his rod hateth his son: but he that loveth him chasteneth him betimes." If you do not discipline your children effectively, *you hate them.* If you do not discipline them in accordance with God's Word, I do not care what your emotional framework is—you are not loving them. Love is defined, not by our emotional framework, but by what the Bible says. Hatred is defined by what the Bible says, and the Bible says that if you do not discipline your kids, it is functionally disowning them—and that includes disowning them by doing nothing more than whumphing the diapers.

So ineffective discipline is a way of disowning, rejecting, or hating your children. God does not do that with us, and we must not do that with our children. At the same time, we want to correct our children while we exhibit all the fruit of the Spirit. That's why disciplining children is the Christian life in microcosm. It is not some secular pursuit detached from issues like sin and forgiveness, gospel and redemption. Child discipline is all about Jesus. We are nurturing souls, not training puppies. This is a form of discipleship and ministry, and it cannot be ministry without Jesus being at the center of it.

You do not earn your justification by undergoing discipline. Sanctification does not drive you into justification, and you do not find your position in Christ because someone spanked you into your position with Christ. You were adopted by God's free grace. Then God puts one of the marks of your membership in His family on you: He chastens every son He has. So take *heart*. God is loving you when He disciplines you. You receive the gift of sanctifying discipline as a result of free grace.

When I was disciplined as a boy, my dad was always judicious and calm and would give us an opportunity for the defense, which was generally pretty thin. He would discipline and then hold us, pray with us, and say something like this: "Everything is completely and totally forgiven, and you can come back and rejoin the family, a full participating member of it, as soon as you are prepared not to be sulky about it." I can remember sitting down in the basement, listening to the happy clink of silverware upstairs, like the prodigal son in the far country.

When this happened, before I repented and rejoined the family, was I a Wilson? I was as much a Wilson on the basement steps as any other time in my life. In fact, that is *why* I was there. My dad did not do that with the neighbor kids (as tempting as that might have been at times). I was there *because* I was a Wilson. My family membership was never more secure than when I was sitting there, disciplined.

Was I happy about being a Wilson? Not necessarily. So you are a justified Christian. It is your status as a Christian. And then God disciplines, scourges, and corrects. He does different things that introduce troubles into our lives, and if we get angry or upset, it is like we are sitting on the basement steps refusing to rejoin the family. You are welcome to come back upstairs anytime, and learn the lesson from it. When you learn the lesson, when you see how your sanctification relates to your justification, then you can see how the discipline of your children portrays that as well. Your theology of justification and sanctification is coming out your fingertips, especially if you are disciplining your children.

PART THREE

NURTURE
AND
ADMONITION

CHAPTER 8

THE NECESSITY OF A CHRISTIAN *PAIDEIA*

And, ye fathers, provoke not your children to wrath:
but bring them up in the nurture
and admonition of the Lord.

EPHESIANS 6:4

I
n the previous section we distinguished
discipline from punishment. That initial
distinction was that discipline is corrective, and punishment is concerned simply with

justice or retribution. When a magistrate executes a criminal, he is not trying to make that criminal better, but is simply executing justice. It may or may not make that criminal better, but the point is not disciplinary, but rather punitive. What parents do in the household is disciplinary, not punitive.

Once we have accepted the duty of administering parental discipline, we discover that discipline itself falls into two categories: corrective and formative. Corrective discipline is correction of manifested sins in the past, as well as correction with regard to the future. Formative discipline anticipates temptations that are common to man and seeks to instill certain character traits beforehand.

In this text, the charge is given to fathers. Taking all of Scripture together, we know that both fathers and mothers are engaged in this crucial task (for example, in the book of Proverbs, a young man is exhorted to obey the law of his *mother*). At the same time, it is worth noting that the central charge in this passage is delivered to the father. God commands to our weaknesses. Mothers and wives generally do not need to be exhorted to be interested and invested in the day-to-day ongoing education of their children. Fathers do need to be exhorted in this way, and so Paul does precisely that.

We are also taught just a few verses before this that the husband is the head of the wife as Christ is the head of the Church, and this means that the father is responsible for everything that goes on in the household. He is responsible, in the first instance, not to be a provocation to his children. Again, God commands to our weaknesses. When the Bible says, "Fathers don't do that" or "Wives don't do this" or "Children don't do that," God is speaking to things that we might possibly do if we were not exhorted to avoid it. So fathers do have a tendency to provoke their children, and the apostle is countering this. When a father stumbles his children into wrath, his sin is prior to theirs and is much more grievous. In Luke 17:2, Jesus says it would be better for a man to have a millstone tied around his neck than to stumble one of these little ones.

Now the father of the family is required to provide his children with a Christian education and upbringing. Christian children should receive much more than a Christian education, but at the very least they should receive a Christian education. The words translated in Ephesians 6:4 as "nurture and admonition" are *paideia* and *nouthesia*. They are almost synonyms, so it is hard to tell which word is translating which word. Each word could be rendered "nurture," and each word could be rendered "admonition." Take them together, and they encompass and necessarily require a Christian education.

What we mean by education is not as big as this charge is, but it is necessarily a critical component of it. When we say Christian education, everyone thinks schools, history, geography, or math. We think of this as the particular "formal" time that is set aside, but while *paideia* does include that formal schooling time, it is not limited to that.

Nowadays, education is thought of as "data-dumping," but raw requirement without instruction is a form of provocation. But on the other hand, parents should not allow their kids to dodge obedience with requests for explanation. "Why do we have to do it?" It is a parental obligation to answer those questions, but I also think a shrewd parent will say, "I tell you what. Those are all great questions. Why

THE NECESSITY OF A CHRISTIAN PAIDEIA 57

don't you clean the garage like I told you to, and when you finish, we'll sit down and go over why I had you do that." All of a sudden it appears that the child does not really want answers to the questions; all he wants to do is delay cleaning up the garage. You do not want requests for explanation to displace obedience.

At the same time, if your child routinely hears nothing more than "because I said so," and they have no idea why they are being shepherded in this direction, something is drastically wrong. The two halves of this verse are connected. It says, "Fathers, provoke not your children to wrath, but bring them up in the nurture and admonition of the Lord." Teaching them, instructing them, walking alongside them, and making the world make sense to them all are ways of not provoking your children to wrath.

One of the ways fathers provoke their children to wrath is by not equipping them. They are not equipped to work hard, to do higher levels of math, to hold down a job, to respond well to authority . . . but by the time that happens, they often realize that the train left the station and it's too late. They are not equipped. Who was it that did not equip them? If Dad does not provide a godly Christian education, then he has neglected to do what Paul is teaching in this passage.

You've read this important point about discipline a couple times already, but it applies to Christian *paideia* as well. So here it is again: The difference between corrective and formative discipline is that when something has gone actively wrong, corrective discipline puts things back on track, restoring the fellowship between parent and child, while formative discipline prevents things from going wrong in the future. All discipline is corrective, but some discipline corrects past mistakes and other discipline prevents future mistakes.

Suppose Mom told her son on her way out the door that she wanted him to get his math homework done before playing any video games. Suppose he gets into a junior-high-boy-rationalization mode and starts thinking about how much math was involved in programming video games and that in fact the spirit of math is *suffused* through these video games! When, later that evening and all of a sudden, his explanations and rationalizations vanish as the morning dew and the consequences fall on him, his mom is imposing the first kind of discipline, corrective discipline concerning an incident in the past.

The second kind of discipline is the exercise of having to do the math homework in the first place. When children are given math homework, they might feel persecuted. They have been given the pile of work, not because they have done anything wrong, but because their parents want them to continue to not do wrong throughout the course of their lives. Math homework is an example of equipping your children for a future day, and this is formative discipline. It is corrective also, but it is preventative correction. This is the same with other subjects. You are anticipating common problems, and you are equipping your child to protect against that day. This connects to the whole issue of character formation.

One writer has helpfully noted that education is about *formation*, not so much *information*. Preventative correction, done right, is a character-building process. One of the grand mistakes parents often make is that of opposing academics to character issues. Learning to do the kind of work that children have learned to do and have had to learn to do for millennia is not opposed to character formation—it *is* character formation. If a group of boys were working with shovels in order to dig a ditch, and the father of one of the boys came out to pull his boy aside to spend the morning doing something other than digging, this would not be an example of focusing on character instead of digging a ditch.

While character is more important than the ditch, if you don't dig the ditch, you don't get the character. What you get is someone who leans on his shovel or goes home and sits on the sofa. *All* of the tasks in front of us are character-building opportunities. Taking your kid home from his ditch-digging job would be an example of refusing to work on character.

CHAPTER 9

PRINCIPLES AND METHODS

W e cannot talk about these matters without talking about principles and methods. Imagine a four-lane highway, with two lanes going opposite ways, two to Heaven, two to Hell. A Ford and a Chevy are on the two lanes going to Heaven, and on the two lanes going to Hell are a Ford and a Chevy. We live in a perverse time, such that when the Fords pass, the drivers beep and wave at each other. Same thing with the Chevys. The cars going in different directions might feel a real sense of solidarity, since they have the same kind of vehicle, but they are going in completely different directions.

When it comes to education, some people go to private Christian schools, some people home school, and some people use co-ops. As with the Ford/Chevy analogy, it does not matter nearly so much what kind of vehicle you are driving as where you are driving it. There are people who are making *different* choices for good and godly reasons that have far *more* in common than someone who is making the same choices but for completely different reasons. The choice itself is not as important as the reasoning. We do not want to fall into stupid Ford-Ford or Chevy-Chevy alliances. We want to think about the principle—are we bringing up our children in the nurture and admonition of the Lord? If your primary loyalty is to the method, you are not thinking like a Christian. If your primary loyalty is to the goal, you will find yourself in good fellowship with a number of people who are pursuing the same goal with different methods.

But what is the goal? The word *paideia* that Paul uses in Ephesians 6:4, which we discussed in the previous chapter, is an enormous word. Every language has comprehensive words like that—in our culture an example of this would be the word "democracy." It is so important to our culture that you would not be astonished to find a three-volume study of that word in a used-book store. *Paideia* was one of those huge words in the ancient world, and it referred to the enculturation of a child so that he could take his place as a citizen in the polis. In other words, *paideia* referred to an all-encompassing, civilization-making reality. Paul is using the word to refer to something very similar. The apostle Paul saw Christians as at one time being aliens from the commonwealth of Israel (cf. Eph. 2:12), but later taking their place as citizens of the new Jerusalem (cf. Gal. 4:26; Heb. 12:22). He refers to the same thing in Philippians when he talks about our citizenship being in heaven (Phil. 3:20). A Christian *paideia* prepares a child for their adult responsibilities as a citizen in the kingdom of God. When Paul requires fathers to provide a Christian *paideia*, he requires this before there was any such thing as a Christian culture for the children of the first Ephesians who received this letter.

The injunction to bring children up in the *paideia* of the Lord is staggering, especially since

there was no Christian civilization to encultur-
ate them into. What was he telling the Ephesians
to do? In order to fulfill his requirement here,
the earlier Christians had to build such a culture, which they subsequently did—and this is
why we are here today. Western civilization is
the result of that endeavor. It is not synonymous
with that endeavor, and the kingdom of God is
not Western civilization, but there is no possible
way to tell the story of the one without telling
the story of the other. You cannot tell the story of the history of the Church without telling
of Charlemagne and Alfred the Great, and you
cannot talk about Western civilization without
talking about the early Church fathers.

As we continue to fulfill this obligation, the
goal is to have civilization and the kingdom of
God become more and more synonymous and
harder and harder to tell apart. Right now, it
is pretty easy to tell them apart. Currently, the
battle between light and darkness is obvious.
It was even more obvious when Ephesians was
written. Nonetheless, the early Christians did
what the apostle Paul told them to do, and the
end result was a Christianized culture. They
did not do so perfectly, and we are not even

close to being done yet, but they did create a Christian culture in which it was possible to educate their children. We are privileged to have significant aspects of what they built still functioning as part of our heritage, which means that we do not have to start from scratch the way they had to.

There are many endeavors that Christians ought to pursue with that great two-word prayer, which is "Geronimo! Amen." God is the one who is superintending the whole process. But when we do this, we have to trust the Lord, knowing that we only know one tiny fraction of everything that is going on, even when it comes to what's going on with our own children. Consequently, we simply have to receive God's Word and pursue it to the best of our ability as God enables us by His grace.

CHAPTER 10

CHILDREARING AND COMMUNITY

W hen children are little, parents can fall prey to the grip of an idea—all kinds of fantastical notions about education stratagems, health weirdness, child discipline, food phobias, and so on. For much of this stuff, we can and should say, with the apostle Paul, that every man should be convinced in his own mind (Rom. 14:5). One of the ways we keep peace in our diverse congregation is we let other people do it their own way. This is a good and proper thing to do. However, we also need to remember that it is not wise to live in an echo chamber (2 Cor. 10:12). If nobody can approach you and question your decisions, you have an ungodly attitude. You should be fully convinced in your own mind at the end of the day because you need to make the decisions for your family, but you must be open to input from others.

If you have never seen a godly example of parents bringing up their children, spend some time seeking it out with caution. When you seek out godly advice and godly examples to imitate, be careful. We learn by imitation but we also envy by imitation. You have to learn how to copy without comparing.

One of the great truths that I discovered by building my house was the nature of concrete work. The one bright spot about concrete work is that a couple of hours after you pour, no matter what, you are all done. You do not have to ever worry about having to stay up late into the night to finish the work.

Your children are that wet concrete. This does not obligate you to a particular course of action, but it does obligate you to a certain demeanor. The people surrounding you have an obligation to help you in the Christian nurture of your child. We are not in the realm of Hillary Clinton's "it takes a village to raise a child," but in a limited sense, your children are members of a covenant people and a congregation. It is quite possible—certain, in fact—that some parents sitting across the aisle might know more about what's going on with you and your kid than you do. You might not know that your kid is a pill, and the person sitting across from you at church might not know your kid's middle name—but he can still see that the kid is a pill. We need people to be looking at the back of our head.

When you are told to bring up your children in the *paideia* of the Lord, this means that you are to bring them up so that they are incorporated into a larger body that is bigger than your family. Not only is it bigger than your family, but the Church of God is more important than your family. You are not obligated to do whatever anybody says, but you *are* obligated to be willing to hear about it without getting your back up. Psalm 141:5 says this: "Let the righteous smite me; it shall be a kindness: and let him reprove me; it shall be an excellent oil, which shall not break my head." At the end of the day, you do have the liberty in Christ to differ with your brothers and sisters when they come to you about something they see. However, you do not have the right to get upset when they have a different perspective on it than you do. You do not have the right to automatically blow them off.

We are involved in one another's lives, and this is handy, because certain sins and blunders run out ahead of you and others trail behind (1 Tim. 5:24). Parental folly is the kind of thing that can have a long fuse—one of your brothers in Christ might see something coming a decade before it happens. You have to surrender to the Lord, take it before the Lord, ask God about it . . . and be willing to consider it. Proverbs 12:1 says, "Whoso loveth instruction loveth knowledge: but he that hateth reproof is brutish." You can tell whether you are instilling the right kind of discipline in your children by how *you* respond when someone suggests something to you. If you get your back up when anyone suggests something to you, you cannot be surprised when your child gets his back up when you suggest something to him. He is learning how to be teachable from you. Or not.

CHAPTER 11

ONLY ONE HIDING PLACE FROM SIN

Y ou are to bring your children up to take their position among their people, and that means success is found in them going away. As it says in Genesis, a man will leave his father and mother and cleave to his wife and the two become one flesh. It is a design feature for them to establish a new household. In *The Four Loves*, C.S. Lewis comments on the kind of need-love that refuses to let go. That is not successful childrearing. Childrearing is preparation for life in the kingdom of God as it interacts with the kingdom of man.

What happens in the Christian school family or in the homeschool community is not supposed to be happening in isolation. When we are preparing our people to go out into the congregation, the people out there are oftentimes sinful and unreasonable, and that means your kid is going to get mistreated. Somebody is going to say something to your kid that they ought not to say. So? Welcome to earth, kid. We are not supposed to bring up our children wrapped in cotton padding or sealed in bubble wrap where they never encounter sin.

People have asked me, "Why on earth did you send your kids to Logos School?" I did it because there is so much sin there. That's a great reason to send them there. There are hundreds of kids, and they sin up a storm—and the teachers and the administrators are descended from Adam, too. We have all kinds of problems. But what we also have is a community where we have committed ourselves to deal with sin scripturally. There is no place on the planet where you can hide your kids from the presence of sin.

If you locked your children in a cabin on top of a mountain in western Montana to educate them there, you would find that our common father Adam has followed you up the mountain and is going to start manifesting his presence in all sorts of ways. Sin has to be addressed with gospel, not with isolation or defensive padding.

This is a challenge, because when you have your children in a catechism class or school, or when you are in a co-op, and a teacher did not teach correctly or treat your kid the way they ought to have, then you and your child are getting the kind of preparation for Christian living that you need. Hiding from the sin out there will not protect us from the sin in here. There are people out there with blind spots and vendettas. There are people with good intentions that go wrong, and you cannot hide from that truth. You have to confront it with gospel and go straight at it.

We must equip our children to meet this kind of thing with a gospel heart. You must equip your children with gospel, and teach them to identify with their brothers and sisters at church, despite the fact that we are not on the same page in every respect. This is what it means to build community and live together. This brings us back to the touchstone of grace. The only place to hide from sin is in Jesus Christ. Every other technique will not and cannot work. You must be trusting in Jesus. If you are pursuing a particular educational method while you are trusting in Jesus, God is going to bless those efforts. If you think you have got it covered, then your method is not under the blessing of God, and it is going to come apart in your hands. It does not matter what it is or who is involved.

You can have the best equipment in the world, but if you try to make an omelet with rotten eggs, you are still going to get a rotten omelet. It doesn't matter how good the recipe is, or how fancy the kitchen is. In order to not have rotten eggs, you have to have Jesus—forgiveness, cleansing, humility, and confession of sin. That is why when Christians get on their high horse about different methods of education, it is spiritually dangerous, not because they are necessarily wrong about the method, but because their attitude excludes Jesus. When you do that, you are forfeiting the blessing. You should only want to undertake the work of bringing up your children, teaching and educating them, if the whole thing is on the altar waiting for the fire to fall.

PART FOUR

MORE LIKE CHRIST

CHAPTER 12

IMITATE ME

*For though ye have ten thousand instructors in Christ,
yet have ye not many fathers: for in Christ Jesus I
have begotten you through the gospel. Wherefore I
beseech you, be ye followers of me. For this cause have
I sent unto you Timotheus, who is my beloved son,
and faithful in the Lord, who shall bring you into
remembrance of my ways which be in Christ, as I teach
every where in every church.*

1 CORINTHIANS 4:15–17

Be ye followers of me, even as I also am of Christ.

1 CORINTHIANS 11:1

B iblical parenting is much more than a bag of tips and techniques. Techniques are helpful if you are learning to paint by numbers, but this is not the kind of thing that we are doing when bringing up children. At the same time, it is not so mysterious and so out of this world that you cannot figure out what you are doing. We are not in a blind fog through which we can only helplessly grope. Wise parents understand what they are doing, but it is not mechanical.

Godly parenting is a function of becoming more like Jesus in the presence of little ones who are also in the process of becoming more like Jesus. Both of you are learning lessons in the school of sanctification. In this book on childrearing we have talked about justification, which establishes the fact of your relationship with God, and sanctification, which is the process of directing that relationship. In the school of sanctification, the parents are in the upper grades and the kids are in the lower grades. Where the kids are, the parents once were, and where the parents are now, the children will be.

We can see the principles laid out in the Word, and we have to obey them, but we must not imitate them as though trying to manufacture childrearing techniques out of 2x4s. Childrearing does not work that way. Childrearing is not impossible and does involve rule-guided behavior, but it must always be personal. Recall Part One: The word translated as "follower" is *mimetai*, from which we get the words "mimic" and "mime." In 1 Cor. 4:15-17, we learn that genuine Christian discipleship is driven by a paradigm that is much more like a family than a lecture hall. It is like a father talking to his children around a dinner table. It is like a mother speaking to her daughter in the kitchen as they discuss something that is very important to her.

Parenting is not like a data dump, a book, or a lecture. Those may be valuable in their place, but they do not quite fit the bill when you are bringing up children. They are valuable in their place, and good as far as they go, but they are not the whole thing.

Paul says in 1 Corinthians 4:15 that one father is tantamount to ten thousand instructors. If you do not have a dad, it does not matter how many lectures you get. One of the things that we are dealing with in our culture today is a crisis of fatherlessness. We are trying to fix it with ten

thousand instructors, but it is going to take a lot
more than that. So for that reason, Paul pleads
for the Corinthians to be imitators of him (v.
16). He tells them to copy him, to watch what
he does, and to do the same thing. This rubs
us the wrong way because we are individualists,
and we want to be original. We want to do our
own thing and to march to our own drum, but in
reality everyone is copying somebody.

Either you are going to copy someone who
grows you into yourself, or you are going to copy
someone in a way that creates a lot of problems.
This is why Paul sent Timothy: he was a beloved
son of Paul. The son could remind them of his
father's ways.

In 1 Corinthians 11 we learn that when we
are imitating Paul, we are imitating an imitator.
Paul is himself imitating Christ (1 Cor. 11:1).
The original pattern was not set by Paul but
rather by the Lord Jesus. He imitated Christ and
so we are to imitate him; to the extent that Paul
is imitating Jesus, we are to be imitating Paul.
One of the central things that we must imitate
is this pattern of imitation itself.

There are, of course, two types of imitation.
True progress and godliness is something that

develops through imitation, but because human beings are necessarily imitators, the same thing is true of ungodliness. We are born into this world as sinful descendants of Adam, so we have a certain bent towards the imitation of the ugly and the sinful, and we will keep that bent until the Lord converts us. But even then, whether we are imitating God or sinners, we are growing by imitation. We are constantly in danger of envying other people and comparing ourselves to them, but if the whole process is occurring in Christ, then we are safe.

One way to tell whether you are copying in a wise way or in a foolish way is this: when we are imitating biblically, the more we do it, the more we become like ourselves. The more like Christ you become, the more your personality will shine forth. We see situations where someone copies someone else and loses himself as a result, but that is because of what I call ego comparison. If it is envy-driven or comparison-driven, we will get more and more tangled up. However, when we all become like Jesus and all the billions of believers are gathered around the throne of God, it will not be an army of clones that can only be distinguished one from another by the serial number on the bottom of their foot.

The more like Jesus you are, the more like yourself you are going to be. The less like Jesus you are, the more monotonous and predictable it's going to be. Sin is monotonous. Godliness is not.

The more someone *copies* their dad self-consciously in Christ, the more unique a father he becomes. When we try to preserve our originality by being as unique and cool as possible, what is actually going on is that we are copying other people with sidelong glances and we are unable to admit to ourselves that that is what we are doing. I recall something I learned from *Mad Magazine* back in the 60s: "Today's non-conformists are getting harder and harder to tell apart." When you copy with the sidelong glance, what you are doing is invisible to you. *You do not know* that you are just like everyone else. But if you copy the people God tells you to copy, and you imitate them as they imitate Christ, then you are not about to lose yourself. Rather you are in the process of becoming what God meant you to be.

CHAPTER 13

PARENTS WORTH IMITATING

W e are all familiar with the jibe that's embedded in the saying, "Do as I say, not as I do." When parents are confronted with a challenge, their first reaction should not be, "Let's put a stop to this," or "Sin has appeared in our child! We must whack it!" Rather, the first reaction should be to prayerfully ask if the Lord is revealing something to you about your own behavior and your pattern of life.

If you ask, "Where did our little Sally pick this up?" and you assume it is from some reprobate down the street on the playground, you should stop and consider that perhaps they are picking it up from you. Is it possible that in this situation, God is holding up a mirror to you so that you would begin your correction of them by repenting of your own sin?

Let us consider some examples of this. Suppose a child is guilty of bad manners at the table and his father snaps at him. The child has bad manners, sure enough, and his father told him not to have those bad manners. But why does he have bad manners at the table? *Because his father does.* Snapping at your children at the dinner table is much worse than playing with your potatoes with a knife. The Word of God never says anything about playing with your potatoes with a knife, but it *does* address the root sin of biting someone else's head off. Dad is disobeying the Bible and doing so in a way that humiliates everybody there, including the child who is playing with potatoes.

It is not okay for children to play with their food, but that is because it is good manners to avoid that sort of thing. However, it is far worse to be cracking down on bad manners with *uber-*bad manners. This is an instance where the parents have essentially said bad manners are accepted and tolerated at this table. The children have clearly got a problem with playing with the potatoes—but bad manners are absolutely okay. The parents have just displayed them.

Here is a more positive example. Instead of a father saying, "Go help your mother clean the table," he says instead, "Come, let's help your mother clear the table." He sets the pattern. I do not mean to say it is always wrongheaded for a parent to tell a child to go do something. Life is not possible unless kids are sometimes assigned missions. But they should be assigned a mission that they have seen routinely modeled for them by their parents.

If there is one thing that you take away from this little book it should be this: parents have a tendency to mislabel the lesson. If you have ever been in a Bible study trying to track with the lesson when everyone else is in 1 Kings and you are in 2 Kings, then the more you try, the more awkward it gets. If they are doing one thing and you are doing something completely different, you are going to get completely muddled.

Imagine a basic showdown scenario: suppose a toddler is standing at the coffee table right across from you and repeatedly wants to mess with the vase. Suppose further that the toddler has just gotten mobile and you have not child-proofed the house yet, and they keep wanting to touch the vase. Too often, parents think that the lesson is entitled "How not to mess with vases," when the *actual* lesson is called "How not to get exasperated with other people." You are teaching the toddler how not to get exasperated with other people when they cross you repeatedly, and that is the real lesson you are teaching them.

How does God teach us? Hosea 11:3 says that God taught Ephraim to walk the way a parent would teach a child, standing behind them and taking them by the arms. That is how we teach our children to walk when they are just getting mobile. What is going on? When you are in this scenario across the coffee-table from your toddler, your job is not to teach the child to be a child. We sometimes think our child is deficient because he wants to touch the vase and we have to transform the child into somebody who does not want to touch the vase. But your task is not to teach the child how to be a child—the child already knows how to be a child. You are not teaching your children to be children. You are teaching your children to grow into adults.

This is why, when you are in this showdown across the coffee table, you should look into the future with the eye of faith and see your child standing where you are now standing and their children standing where he is now standing. And how will he know how to deal with his son? He will have learned how from you!

If you do not know how to be patient in the face of repeated provocations, your children are not going to know either. When you discipline your children correctly, *you are loving your grandchildren*. Your job is not to teach them to be an acceptable child, but to show them how to be a responsible adult—because that is the whole point.

Be honest—you bought the vase at a yard sale last summer and that vase is going to be in another yard sale this coming summer. Who cares about the vase? The child is going to live forever. The child is not something you acquired or are going to get rid of in a yard sale. The vase is. You are not teaching the child to be a good version of what they are. You are rather teaching them to be what they are becoming. What are you going to be?

This principle does not change. Suppose you are dealing with an obstinate teenager and you are thinking "How to fix the teenager" is your task for the day. Your job is not to fix the teenager. Your task is to model for that teenager how to be a parent. Your teen, in just a few short trips around the sun, is going to have a teenager of her own. You are not training her to be a teenager. She has that down already. You are preparing her for the day when she won't be.

The same thing goes for teachers. The lesson plans that you made up and turned in to administration are not the real lesson. The real lesson is modeling Christ for the students, loving Christ and loving the student and loving the material. That is what godly teaching is. When the students see you interacting with them and with the material as someone who loves Jesus Christ, that has a profound impact. If you are doing something else, it has an impact also, but not a good one.

There are also many occasions when imitation is right on the surface. It is harder to keep your kids from smoking if you smoke. It is harder to keep them from anger if you are constantly angry yourself. But there is another way of opening the way to ungodly imitation, even if your kids never see you doing something wrong. God is present, remember, and God sees what doors you are opening in your household, even the secret doors, and what locks you are leaving unlocked, even the secret locks.

For example, a father with a secret porn habit cannot be shocked to discover that his son develops the same problem, even if his son never saw his father doing it. What is happening is that the father is granting some form of covenantal permission. He is saying, "In this household, we leave those doors unlocked. It's alright to be lackadaisical about it." Secret sin can be imitated also. There is a deep structure to this that we cannot pretend to understand, but it is remarkable how this sort of thing can run in lines, even if it is not done openly.

When we pray, think, or meditate on what it is to bring up children, it is tempting to come to the end and say, "Well, all you need is love." Oddly enough, this truism is actually true, but not really the way the Beatles meant it. The Bible tells us in 1 John 4:8 that God is love. God is Lord over all things, and His way of loving is connected wonderfully and authoritatively to absolutely everything. In other words, there is no place you can go in this world where love is irrelevant. Love is always relevant because God is love. It is in Him that we live and move and have our being. God is the Lover, Jesus is the Beloved, and the Love between them is the Spirit. It is in the Triune Love that we live and move and have our being.

This means that love is relevant everywhere. This explains why if we detach love from whatever it is we are doing, the result is spiritual bankruptcy. If I have mastered all the parenting techniques but have not love, I am nothing. Godly teaching, character formation, and discipleship are simply this—loving God and loving the thing you are doing currently in the presence of another person whom you also love. Love God, love what you are doing, and love who you are doing it with. If you do that, Jesus Christ is present. If you are not doing that, it does not matter if you say, "Let's forget about Him. After all, I've got a checklist." You have to do what you do *in Christ*.

Imagine a father and a son in the presence of an unsplit cord of wood. What is the father's duty? His duty is to take two axes, hand one of them to his son, and to love God and to also love a morning of splitting wood, and to do so alongside his son whom he also loves. That is what godly childrearing is.

Love God, love what you are doing, and love the people God gave you to do it with. Does that remove the need to correct? No, you have to show them how to hold the ax and keep them from swinging it around carelessly. Correction, discipline, teaching, mentoring—all of it must be there because you love Jesus, because you love the wood, and because you love your son. That is what you must do.

CHAPTER 14

IMITATE CHRIST

I t is a common devotional exercise for people to go through 1 Corinthians 13, inserting their own name everywhere it says love. What you actually need to do is go through it and put the name of Jesus in there. Jesus is patient, Jesus is kind. Jesus does all these things perfectly, and I must do what I am doing in Him.

If you are not imitating Him or imitating people who imitate Him, if you are correcting your children harshly or blindly with a sense of panic, or if you are not correcting your children as you ought, then it is very easy to think back upstream and believe that God is doing the same thing with you. Some of you parents may have read this book feeling like you are being repeatedly kicked in the head. You may feel like there is nothing you can do about it—your kids are all older, and it seems like God is looking at you the way you used to look at your kids.

But God is not like that with you. When you think of the omniscient, omnipresent God, you need to think of a *Father*. Too many of us think of Him as an omniscient, omnipresent, omnipotent force or power like electricity, only with a mean streak that is going to get us. But He is not like that at all, and you failed because you were thinking He *was* like that. He is going to forgive you. He is going to take you from where you are, not from where you should have been.

You need to say, "Alright, I cannot do any of this outside of Christ. It all has to be in Jesus, in a spirit of love, and I need to turn to Him and accept the forgiveness that He offers, and have Him take me from there." That is what you have to understand. This is not Super-Law. This is all gospel. Childrearing is all gospel because God is bringing *us* up too. And what is He bringing us up to? To His presence, into His joy and into His

Heaven. He is bringing us up to be like Jesus. He is growing us up into ourselves.

QUESTIONS AND ANSWERS WITH DOUG AND NANCY

QUESTION 1

Is there ever a good time to ask your child, "How do you think that makes me feel?"

DOUG: It's either self-pity or rhetorically ineffective.

QUESTION 2

Is there ever a time to ask, "How do you think that makes your mom feel?"

DOUG: It depends. If you want to see the children more grateful or more appreciative for the meals that are cooked, there is nothing wrong with insisting on that, since you're insisting on behalf of another.

NANCY: Of course, you probably shouldn't do that in the middle of the meal. You should try to get them to do it afterwards, or you should prepare them ahead of time, instead of guilt-tripping the kids. Doug helped me learn not to take the kids' disobedience personally. If I got offended, it muddied the waters, and I would start attributing motives: "If you loved me, you wouldn't have done that, so there must be some deeper problem!" Just stay objective: "I said not to do this, and you did it anyway." That way it's not about you or your feelings.

DOUG: Going back to the dinner example, instead of saying, "Why are you a bunch of ingrates?" at the table and ruining the dinner, it would be far better to set an example: "This is a wonderful dinner. Don't you think so kids?" Then, if a kid says, "No, this is terrible," that's defiance, and it's a disciplinable moment. However, most of the time when things are good, the kids are just being thoughtless. In those instances, Dad can lead them in showing gratitude.

How do you consistently discipline your child and at the same time show them liberty and freedom?

DOUG: One of the best ways to be consistent is to reduce the number of commandments. For instance, if you have a two-year-old but you also have a house full of things that leave you saying "no touch" all the time, I would recommend you take all the prohibitions that they have and consider how many of them you can eliminate, by baby-proofing the living room, for example. If you reduce all the commands by ninety percent, now it's easier to win every time. If you have a multitude of regulations, then it's going to be hard for the kids to remember them all. I've seen parents who quote commands like they're a machine gun: "Pick up your boots. Put on your coat. Come here. Put that book over there." Eventually they overload and there's going to be some sort of infraction. Also, try to cluster the commands, so you can use the same word each time. For a two-year-old, one of them should be,

"No fussing," and you should make sure that you use the same word every time. If sometimes it's, "No whining," and other times it's "stop being grumpy," you may confuse the child.

QUESTION 4

How do you become a house of *yes* without spoiling your children?

DOUG: God says no because He has a bigger yes. So you might say no to a video, but you then might present them with three pounds of Play-Doh. When a mom says no to a Snickers bar fifteen minutes before dinner, it's a no because she has a yes coming up.

NANCY: One of the things I did when our kids were little was make sure they practiced obedience before I gave them a command. Then, when it was actually time to say no, I could remind them of what I had told them earlier. Then we would just run through it, and I'd say, "Yes, that's perfect! You did it!" Other times I can remember them complaining, and I would tell them to rewind the tape, and go out of the room and then come back in with a cheerful attitude. It's both extending grace and giving them practice.

DOUG: Parents often ambush their kids with commands or requirements, and it's like watching a quarterback get blindsided. Suppose they're playing hot and hard in summertime, and you walk out on the back porch and say, "Time to come in!" Blam! That is just a disobedience factory. It's like having a room full of five kids and bringing one balloon—a little sin balloon. Instead you should go out on the back porch and say, "Kids, ten minutes." That way everybody has a chance to get adjusted; they know it's coming. You're preparing them for success, instead of surprising them so that they're guaranteed to fail. Nancy, you used to train them on the way to the grocery store as well.

NANCY: When we went to the grocery store, I reminded them on the way of three rules: no asking for stuff, no touching anything, and stay with me. It was a game of sorts, and I told them I was proud of them, and several times the cashier would remark about what great kids they were. Obedient and cheerful kids are a good testimony. At the end, if they made it, I always bought them a treat.

QUESTION 5

Can you talk about the steps you took to not take things personally when your children disobeyed?

NANCY: When a child argues, it is tempting to get sucked into the argument. Doug would remind me that I was in authority over our children, and to use that authority wisely. Wisdom doesn't take it personally or get into an argument with the kids.

DOUG: Then it becomes adversarial. You've probably seen refs who start playing the game instead of calling the game. Parents are refs. When they've got the black and white striped shirt on, they are not supposed to be playing in the game. Once you step down and start playing it, it becomes personal and your judgment gets clouded.

NANCY: Sometimes I would be too hasty to say no: "Mom, may I have a cookie?" "No, you may not." Then they would want to argue. So, I had to learn to pause and say, "Well, let me think about it." Often, if I thought about it, I would say yes, or have another idea. I think that it is natural for kids to argue and want to debate with Mom. And so from the early years, Doug would remind me to stay calm in authority over them. Doug had my back, so if they were insubordinate to me, they were insubordinate to him. And he would back me up.

DOUG: And that goes back to what my dad taught me: no disrespecting your mother. I knew when I was dealing with my mother, I was dealing with my father. I wanted my kids to know if they were dealing with Nancy, they were dealing with me. This helped her so she didn't feel the weight of it all. She could just hand it off to me if things got intense or difficult.

QUESTION 6

What steps did you both take to be on the same page when it came to disciplining your children?

DOUG: The Bible tells us that all Christians are to strive for like-mindedness, so a husband and wife ought to be like-minded when it comes to discipline and the standards of obedience. I don't ever recall us having to work hard at that, since Nancy was eager for us to be on the same page. However, there's another important side to this:

little kids need dads to be tough on them, and little kids need moms to not be. There's a nurturing, welcoming aspect that Mom needs to give, and there's a suck-it-up-kid, don't-bleed-on-the-carpet aspect that Dad can provide. Because of this, disagreements can arise when the man thinks the wife ought to be just like him, or when the wife thinks the husband ought to be just like her, instead of recognizing this is a Body-life thing, and God gave kids a Dad so they could learn to be tough, and God gave sons a Mom so they would not have to be tough all the time.

NANCY: If I thought Doug was too hard on somebody or if he let something go and I wondered about it, I wouldn't bring it up in front of the kids. We would talk about it later, out of their hearing so that we would present a united front. Trying to divide us was an automatic spankable offense. If a child asked me for something, and I said no, he was not allowed to go ask Doug. One parent's no was as good as both.

Also, dads tend to be harder on the boys, and softer on the girls. Moms tend to be harder on the girls, softer on the boys. Knowing this tendency can help us be more judicious across the board.

DOUG: And talk about it. When you are not in the trenches with the little kids, be sure to look at the game film. When the kids are all in bed, make sure you talk. "How did that go? How did the day go? How are you feeling about your relationship with so-and-so? How did that incident play out? Okay, next time our plan is going to be this."

QUESTION 7

What did leading devotions with the kids look like?

DOUG: We did a bunch of different things.

NANCY: When we were first married, day one, Doug opened up the Bible and started reading it aloud to me in the morning.

DOUG: Then when kids started coming and schedules got disrupted, we shifted to dinner time. Whether it was reading the Bible, or using a catechism for discussion, or reading a Bible storybook, it happened between dinner and dessert. Then when the kids got older and were in school, the entire dinnertime was taken up with biblical ethics and talking about situations at school. At this point the kids were all eager to tell their stories and ask questions. We also did a lot of reading together as a family: lots of *Narnia* and *Lord of the Rings*. I think it would be inaccurate to say we had family worship. We had regular and ongoing interaction with the Bible and the Word of God and different things that brought our Christian faith to bear, but it was not a set liturgy with singing, opening prayer, and reading.

NANCY: They started reading their own Bibles when they could read. We always had evening prayer together. When they hit junior high, Doug started a Bible study for junior high kids, and we adapted to their age.

QUESTION 8

To get really specific for a minute, what are the concerns you have mentioned regarding "security blankets"?

NANCY: Someone gave me a blanket with satin trim for a shower gift. It was so cute because our baby would grab that thing and just rub her face on it all the time. One day I said, "Look, honey, isn't that cute?" and Doug said, "Get that blanket out of our house." I thought he was kidding at first, but he wanted our kids to be secure in us, not in an object like a blanket.

DOUG: Here's a qualifier, and then another example of this. It's not the end the world if your kid has a security blanket or a binky or something, but there are things to watch out for in things like that. For example, recently I was at an airport, and I saw a girls' volleyball team checking in. As we were going through security, I counted just in the line ahead of me six girls who had stuffed animals with them, and I realized that these girls had no security. As parents, we wanted to emphasize and prioritize our relationship and dependence on and interaction with one another. If we saw one of the kids was starting to have a low tank and maybe even starting to act up to get attention, we would confer, and then pour on more attention and affection than usual.

QUESTION 9

How do you prioritize sins or issues to deal with when Dad gets home?

DOUG: Basically, that is something that should be settled in conference. Women oftentimes specialize in what I call "great experiments in telepathy" and "the glance of a thousand meanings," while men specialize in not hearing things that are overtly said in English out loud. Women pay way too much attention to the vibes in the room, and men don't pay attention enough to the things that are explicitly stated or said. The thing to do is not to have that misunderstanding happen in front of the kids. You should talk about it when you are viewing the game film. For example, when obedience would get a little raggedy around the house, we would confer, talk about it, and perhaps decide to tighten things up. We would line up the kids and tell them that there was too much squabbling or fussing or whatever. We would tell the kids we were sorry for letting that happen, and let them know we were going to have a short reign of terror. That meant no warnings, and spankings for all offenses. Usually no spankings were needed because they got the message. They were old enough to know what we were doing.

QUESTION 10

How do you apologize to your kids?

DOUG: Apologizing to the kids was, like so much of this stuff, something I learned from my dad. I remember vividly him apologizing to me for spanking me up the stairs in anger. He had to go out that evening to lead a Bible study, but he went out to the car, and thought, "I can't go to the study in this shape." So he came back in, came upstairs, and sat on my bed, and sought my forgiveness for spanking me in anger. By doing that, a dad is acknowledging that everyone in the household is under authority, which means that the kids can trust Mom and Dad.

QUESTION 11

Any thoughts on television for your kids?

DOUG: We were pretty strict with TV issues when the kids were little. When they got older in junior high, there was some sort of video game thing. We said if they wanted to listen to some music or play a video game, they would earn time in the bank by reading a book. That way they could store up time. There's a difference between entertainment, which is treated like a birthright, as opposed to recreation, which is a sabbath thing. So if you work hard, if you get up early and go out and hit it, and after dinner, you want to put your feet up and watch the game, that's recreation. But if you are standing behind someone at the video store who has ten movies that they are going to go watch this weekend, that's not recreation—that's a vidiot. We didn't want our kids to be doing that, though we also didn't want to be censorious and exclude things outright. We were on the lookout to make sure they didn't displace valuable things like reading. We read together as a family and listened to books on tape in the car on cross-country trips. We didn't have a TV going in the corner regardless of whether anyone was watching it.

When kids get older, they are more intelligent. Don't you have to increase the number of rules in order to keep up?

DOUG: No, you will never keep up. Disobedience can always expand at a more rapid rate than the rules. Instead, you need to cast a wide net.

If you tell your kids not to do something on Wednesday night and then on Thursday night they do it, should the rule still be in place?

DOUG: I would prefer that you refresh it, since it doesn't take much time. You don't want to open up the door for them to say, "I forgot" or "You didn't tell me that." You are creating opportunities for arguments. The book of Proverbs is a father writing to his son, and it is amazing how much repetition goes into it. When you have to repeat yourself, that's not a sign of system failure. I think God designed children to need to be told the same thing over and over again. And if it's done patiently, then you can keep the issue clear. If you told them to not do something fifteen seconds ago, the issue is disobedience. Twenty-four hours gives them all kinds of maneuvering room.

QUESTION 14

How do you adjust to adopted children, especially if you already have kids that know the rules?

DOUG: You need to give it time and let everybody in the family know that you are giving it time. Don't expect the child who just arrived to unlearn everything in twenty-four hours. At the same time you can't let their upbringing hold everybody hostage. Let them know that it is going to be difficult as you get to know them and they get to know you. Be sure to tell the other kids that this is what you're doing.

QUESTION 15

What about spanking older adopted kids?

DOUG: My Dad's rule was that by the time kids are ten or twelve, we should be all done with spanking. We wanted ninety percent of the spankings that the kids received to occur in their first five years, and then just occasional course-correction through the elementary years. By the time they are heading into junior high, we wanted them to be all done.

With adopted children, you've got no telling what their experience is, but even if they don't have any memory of abuse or anything like that, whenever you discipline a child, you are writing a check and you need to have money in the bank for it. Suppose your daughter is nineteen years old and she wants to go out with some schmo, and you say no. You are writing a check for a hundred thousand dollars by saying that, and you need to have that money in the bank. Similarly, when you spank a child, it's a withdrawal. Are there enough emotional deposits—positive affirmations, and so forth—to enable you to do that? If a spanking is a hundred dollars and this kid arrives in your house with ten cents in the bank, then you don't have the money in the account to do that. So I would suggest a period of adjustment. If you have adopted older kids, like eleven or twelve, that's about the time I recommend discontinuing corporal punishment anyway.

QUESTION 16

What would you do if you discontinue spankings at twelve or thirteen?

DOUG: When they're twelve, they are six years away from joining the navy and going off to the Philippines. When they go off to college, they are not going to have to obey your curfew, and they are going to have to tackle the world on their own, so your standards have to be internalized by that point. You need to move from exoskeletal discipline in the early years to the internalization of the standards when the kids are in their teen years, and the way you do that is by allowing real life consequences as opposed to artificial consequences. When a child is three and disobeys you and climbs over the kid gate at the top of the stairs, you don't want them to learn their lesson via real-life consequences.

Instead you introduce little bite-sized, artificial consequences. Spankings, or swats, are tiny, manageable bits of pain that are nothing compared with what the world would do to them. So it's just little tiny things to teach them the principle of "disobedience means pain," but it is pain that doesn't cause their world to fall apart. When they are twelve to eighteen, you are phasing them into real world consequences. If they break the neighbors' window, they pay for it. If they don't show up for work, you have them go visit their employer and walk up to their door and seek their forgiveness for not showing up. It's not full-tilt, real world consequences, but it's measured out and it gets increasingly like the real world the older they get.

QUESTION 17

What if the kid doesn't think the spanking hurt?

DOUG: I would caution you against getting sucked into a whirlpool of spanking spiraling downward. Everybody loses. Spanking should sting and should hurt, but it ought not to be damaging. If your child defies you when you spank him, it's not painful enough for him to not want it to happen again. So instead of having ten spankings with three swats each, it would be far better to have one spanking with ten swats. You want to win decisively in the first round. Wherever you can, keep it simple, keep it short.

Also, since the American Academy of Pediatricians has declared any form of spanking whatsoever to be child abuse, I want to say that there *is* such a thing as physical abuse of children. Beating them up and spanking them too long or too hard so that you damage them is wicked. The fact that people call any form of spanking child abuse does not mean there is no such thing as child abuse or that there is no such thing in conservative Christian circles. You want the spankings to be painful but short and not damaging.

NANCY: Also, we never used our hands. We would use a little paint stirrer or a wooden spoon.

DOUG: I think a hand is too heavy, and it is hitting as opposed to stinging. Also, if you don't know how to spank with your hand, you could hurt yourself and get mad and actually wind up abusing the kid. Hands should be associated with care, protection, feeding, and loving, not attacking.

QUESTION 18

There is an argument mounted in Christian circles that Proverbs 26:3 says the rod is for the back of fools, not for the rear end of toddlers, so aren't those verses about the rod not about childrearing at all?

DOUG: I would be willing to cheerfully grant that the verse is not specifically talking about a switch for a toddler's rear end, but I would offer an *a fortiori* argument. Are the people who are arguing against spanking toddlers for mischief seriously arguing for corporal punishment for teenagers? Proverbs is talking about corporal punishment for some eighteen-year-old teenage delinquent, the kind of kid that wrecks someone's car. In a more sane society, the teenager would be flogged or beaten with a rod, released, and then made to pay restitution. Right now, there are a million people locked up in our dog kennel system of penitentiaries, and we like to pride ourselves on how humane we are. That is demented and twisted. By *flogging* I'm not talking about the inhumane way Jesus was flogged or the way the British navy used the cat-o-nine tails. The Mosaic Law also says that forty strokes was the limit for how much you could flog someone, lest your brother be degraded in your sight (Deut. 25:3). It's a rough system of justice, but it's better than what we have now. Right now we just drive by our penitentiaries; out of sight, out of mind.

If you are fine with corporal punishment for juvenile delinquents or for rowdies or hoodlums, how much more will you accept a judicious application of a mini-rod to a mini-person? Also, I think swats should generally begin after the child is mobile and can get into things. Occasionally you need a flick for a nursing baby, but it should be little things like saying "no biting."

QUESTION 19

How do you get a boy to sit still for extended periods of time in church?

DOUG: Don't expect instant results. When you look at families around the church and they've got five kids in a row sitting and holding their psalters, I bet if you went to those families every one of them could tell you war stories about the years it took to get to that point. Sitting still for school, for church, and for the dinner table is a hard thing for boys to learn, and they need to practice. Make it a game and prepare them by having them sit still for ten minutes. Get them used to the idea so that they know what it means. Also, be sure to give them other things to do quietly, so they can grow into attentiveness at church.

NANCY: Doug didn't sit with us during church because he was the pastor. Once the kids were in middle elementary or so, I had a "no bathroom" rule during church. They would use the restroom before church. Then they had to wait, unless it was a true emergency.

QUESTION 20

It seems like boys are more obviously sinful, ruled by their passions, but girls are just as sinful in a sneaky and manipulative way. What do you do about that?

NANCY: Here's an example: the other day, Rachel was getting three-year-old Blaire ready to go out the door and Blaire started fussing. Rachel said no fussing, but Blaire wanted to fuss. Rachel said, "Blaire, I said no, so you have to control your heart. Show me how you control your heart. What do you do?" Blaire stopped and said, "Smile?" Rachel could run that play because she had trained her. So she could let her practice and try again.

DOUG: And there's an important truth in there. If the child is disobedient and you come down on them, they're learning, "I'm the weak one. My parent is the strong one." You should talk to your daughter and say, "We want you to be a strong woman of God, not a weak woman of God." A girl who listens to herself instead of coaching herself will end up being worked over by whatever comes her way.

Always remember that boys and girls run on different kinds of fuel. Certain things work for both of them, but boys run on respect-fuel and girls run on love-fuel. Little girls flirt and manipulate; little boys brag. If a boy says "Look at me" before he jumps off the diving board, he's clamoring for respect. However, when someone demands respect, the last thing in the world you want to give him is respect. Proverbs 27:2 says, "Let another praise you, and not your own mouth" (ESV), so security in a boy enables him to wait for that praise from someone else. When boys are young, be sure to praise them rather than pulling back from them. Show them respect now so that they aren't constantly craving it later.

For girls, it's a danger sign if they get clingy. If an uncle shows up for Thanksgiving, and it's been eight years since she's seen him, and your little girl is all over his lap looking for attention, the parental reaction should not be "Aw, that's so cute." It ought to be, "Yikes!" The little girl is feeling unlovely because she's not been loved, and she sees herself as a nuisance, or an irritation, and is insecure about it. The more insecure she is about it, the more she needs attention, and the more she needs attention and love, the more she fishes for male attention. For a long time she's a nuisance, but then all of sudden she turns thirteen and magically guys start paying attention. Now she has something to negotiate with and many girls are just clueless about what's happening.

So while they are young, saturate your boys with respect and your girls with love. Love has to do with commitment, security, attachment, sacrifice: "I will be here for you, I will sacrifice for you, I'm connected to you, and I'm going to display that every chance I get." Respect has to do with abilities and achievements. Give your girl hugs and compliments and reassurances and praise. Tell your young boy that he is really strong, that he is really brave, that he is really fast.

What if there's a fight and you don't know who was in sin?

DOUG: That's the sort of situation where I would take the kids to the back room. If it's "Did too!" "Did not!" and I don't have any godly way of sorting this out, but it's clear that they're both in sin, then I would take away the toy or whatever is causing the fight. Then I would explain that they're both in sin and pray with them. When you don't know for certain, don't discipline and spank anyway. As parents, you have a priestly role in the family. You are responsible for the kids, and if you've got a really good hunch, but you don't know for sure, you don't want a miscarriage of justice, since you are teaching your kids how to administer justice. Proverbs 18:17 says one case seems solid until you hear the other side, and if you don't have two to three witnesses and you spank blindly, then you are teaching principles of injustice. You should make it a constant prayer, "Lord, if there is anything that we need to know that we currently don't know in order to shepherd our kids faithfully, please let us know." And I believe that you are praying there from a position of strong authority. If God wants you to know, you'll know.

How would you encourage your children to delight in each other's company?

DOUG: If they are having trouble getting along, don't put them in a room together and say, "Sort it out." That just means you are going to have to go intervene again. Instead, sit down with them and delight in their company. Even if it's just messing with Play-Doh together, you can show them how to delight in one another's company. Be sure to guide their comments: "Do you see what your sister did? Isn't that great?" Praise the sister and get the sister to praise, and then reverse it. Model what you want to see done. You can't do that endlessly, but you should always prime the pump with parental delight that lets the kids see what it is you are after.

When should we say to our Christian friends or family that something seems wrong?

DOUG: There are many factors. First, are you speaking above your pay grade? If your oldest is five years old, and you suspect this parent of a fifteen-year-old is not handling it right, that increases the burden of proof before you say something. Second, how close are you to them? Suppose you're co-workers, and he's ten years older than you and his kids are ten years older than yours, but you're best friends at work. That reduces the burden of proof on whether or not you should say something. As I mentioned in another context, when you go to someone with a concern, you are writing a check. So how much money do you have in that bank?

If you saw them once at church, then I'd say don't volunteer anything. But if it's your brother, and you're really close, and you can talk about anything else except about this, then you need to figure out a way to talk about it. Also, don't show up on their doorstep as the accuser man or as a person full of dogmatic pronouncements. The first thing you should do is ask them if you can talk to them: "I have some questions about how Johnny is doing. Would you mind if I asked you some questions?" If he says no, then shut up and go back and pray about it some more. If he says, "Sure, ask questions," I would encourage you to have the first one or two be genuine questions, not assertions. "I saw this happen: are you aware of it?" rather than, "It looked that way to me, therefore it is." It is really, really hard to argue with questions. If it is delicate, say, "I'm sure you and your wife have thought about this, and are concerned about it and have prayed about it. How are you tackling this? How are you praying about it? How can we pray for you concerning it?" You can talk for a half hour or forty-five minutes without presenting anything that could cause offense. I'm a pastor, so if someone comes to me with a counseling thing, and if we have an hour, a good half of it or more is me asking questions.

QUESTION 24

What's the fundamental thing to do during the time when your kids are wet concrete?

DOUG: The best thing you can do for your kids is enjoy them! Someone said to Nancy one time, "Just wait till you get to the terrible twos." But a friend told her, "Oh no: I call them the terrific twos." It is bedlam, but you should look at your toddlers and be thinking, "This is the best thing ever." Then when they go to kindergarten, you should be saying, "This is just the best." Then when you hit the next stage, "This is just the best. I didn't know that it would keep getting better!"

NANCY: We could do a whole separate talk on all the funny, entertaining things our kids did. Whenever I was gone and Doug was home with the kids, Rachel would say, "Hey, can I cook?" and he'd say, "Sure, go cook something!" I had never heard this story until recently, but Rachel said one time she got out some Ritz crackers and put olive oil on them and put them in the oven. But she forgot about them, and they burned. When she brought them out to show Doug, he ate one! She was quite pleased with that.

DOUG: The key is to roll with it. You don't roll with or honor or bless disobedience, but you should embrace everything else. Don't try to thwart it or keep it from happening.

What method of schooling do you think is best? Homeschooling or private schooling?

DOUG: I would estimate that a third of our church is at Logos School, a third is home-school families, and a third is mixed. In Romans 14, Paul says that there are certain indifferent things, *adiaphora*, that Christians should not fight about. Educational method is one of those things, in my opinion. If you are fully convinced in your own mind, God bless you, and just do what you are going to do, and don't let anybody guilt you into doing something else.

There are advantages and disadvantages both ways. School takes advantage of division of labor: the man who really loves math can teach math, and the woman who likes English can teach English. A homeschooling mom has to do all the lesson plans, as well as everything else. At first all mom has to do is change the diapers of the youngest, keep the second one occupied with blocks, and teach the first one to read. However, five years later, she is preparing history lesson plans, English lesson plans, and math lesson plans. Two years down, she's doing the same thing, and the division of labor is even more difficult. Some parents take it in stride and do a fantastic job, and God bless them. But let's say you're not one of those parents. If it's starting to be too much hay on your fork and you're considering putting them in a school, but you're afraid of blowback from other homeschoolers, then that's a problem.

If you are not just considering the best possible option based on the best available data, and you're just doubling down on the method, no matter the returns later on, then you are just an ideologue. I often distinguish between homers and homeschoolers. Homeschoolers are people who are living before God, and prudentially choosing which method they think best blesses their children. A homer who is ideologically fixated on doing everything at home is a different thing entirely.

On the other side, there are people who use the same school and the same education philosophy I do, and I feel like I have nothing in common with them. Sometimes I feel I have more in common with a homeschooler, even though we're using different methods. I regard it as a point of pastoral pride that we have had a congregation so thoroughly committed to Christian education for so many years, and we haven't had a blow-up over this. There have been head bonks and skirmishes, and we've had to put out fires here and there, but I am so grateful that in this community we have a range of methods that people are pursuing.

QUESTION 26

What do you do about standards that you and your family have, but that extended family or friends don't have?

DOUG: Kids have eyes in their heads. If they have trouble respecting Grandpa, that problem will be exacerbated if you don't talk about the problems with Grandpa. If you say nothing about it, they are left with a clash of cultures that they have to sort out on their own. You should have a time of debriefing in the car on the way home: "Now kids, do you know why we don't do it that way? We love Grandpa and Grandma, and we respect them a lot, but do you see that there are some things that they do that we don't do?" I think that there is a way of walking kids through this that teaches them to salute the uniform where they still honor their grandpa and grandma, while you're maintaining your own standards.

NANCY: Sometimes the grandparents give the kids permission to do something, and the kids say, "Well, I'm going to go ask my parents." Even when the grandparents say, "Oh no, it's fine," it's a good thing when the kids go check anyway.

DOUG: Right. There are some parents who think that the way out of this bad jam is, "I don't want my kids to be brought up the way I was brought up, so I'm going to pull away from my family and we're not going to go visit for Christmas or Thanksgiving." (Just to be clear, we are talking about normal, civilized human beings here; we are not talking about whether you go visit Hell's Angels for Thanksgiving.) Some Christian parents got converted in college, and they say, "We're going to pull away from our parents, so the kids don't have this bad influence." What the kids are learning to imitate is distance between parent and child. When you run into trouble with them, what's the kid's response going to be? Model for your children what you want them to be doing for you. Do you want them to put a priority on getting home during the holidays? The best thing in the world you can do is model that for them.

QUESTION 27

Doug, you're obviously very productive. What are the mechanics of not bringing the work home?

DOUG: I believe in plodding and chipping away, a little bit at a time. It adds up. To put this in perspective, I'm sixty now, and I've written a bunch of books, but my first book was published when I was almost forty. We saw the time when the kids were little as plowing and planting. We spent a lot of time with family, cultivating that relationship with the kids because we saw that our kids were our fundamental qualification to be doing what I wanted to be doing in the first place. Back then there wasn't an internet, or an iPhone, or even a computer.

So we read in the evenings, I coached the kids' teams, and took them on dates. One of the things I wrote in *Wordsmithy* is that if you want to write, you have to have lived a life. There was a good twenty years of building the school, teaching my kids, doing Bible studies with the kids, coming home to the kids. A whole bunch of the stuff that I am currently doing I was not doing then. I was getting ready to do it, and I wanted to do it. I remember vividly that part of our game plan was this: "Moscow is a great place to bring up kids, and that's the priority. We want an intact family. Let's get our kids through high school, and then we'll move to the East Coast and do something there." I wanted to make a dent, but by the time my kids were in high school, desktop publishing had arrived, and we started *Credenda/Agenda*, and I realized that we could do the things I had wanted to do from here.

John Owen wrote a commentary on Hebrews that is seven volumes in 6- or 8-point font, and the first two volumes are the introduction. I wonder what he could have done with a word processor. When I look at Calvin's commentaries on the Bible, and then I look at what he did breaking up fights in Geneva, advising the city council on political issues, and all with the medical problems he had, I sometimes wonder why God didn't give Calvin a well-stocked library and a big stack of blank paper so that he could just write down all his wisdom. But if God had put him in an ivory tower like that, he wouldn't have had anything to say. You need real people, real life, real time. The glory of young men is their strength, but their glory is not their patience. Ninety percent of what I'm doing now, I was not doing then.

NANCY: But we did start a school. You were doing things. There were lots of board meetings. When the school moved into the roller rink, they had to completely remodel it. So we have had times we call "hunker down times," and that was one of them. One night Doug got home at eleven, and I remember saying, "Wow, you're home early!" But most of the time he was still home for dinner. Doug and Nate also built most of our house. And they did that in the summers. Nate was in eighth grade when they started, and it took us a while, so that was a lot of their one-on-one time.

DOUG: That was the shop class that neither of us had ever had at school.

QUESTION 28

Did you do Daddy dates?

DOUG: Generally, when the kids were little, Saturday morning was my time to take the kids out, which would give Nancy time off. She would stay home, and I would take the kids as a group.

NANCY: It usually involved donuts and the library and Moscow Mountain.

DOUG: When I took the kids out, generally, the house stayed calm. But when Nancy went out...

NANCY: I would find socks everywhere when I got home.

DOUG: I have to explain a game we had: I would have the kids pull out a sofa, and we'd go gather up every sock in the house and roll them all up in little balls. I would sit in this chair across the room, and then the kids had to walk behind the couch with a slipper on their head. The game was to see if I could knock the slipper off. That was such a blast. But then Nancy would come home...

NANCY: Well, they'd put all the socks away, but I would find them for days or weeks in odd places. And of course we did jammy rides.

DOUG: Jammy rides were when the kids were smaller—pre-school to elementary school age. We'd do the normal bedtime thing, singing and praying, and put them all to bed. And after they'd been in bed ten minutes, I'd yell, "Jammy ride!" and everybody would hop up, run out, and get in the car in their PJ's. Then we'd go to Baskin Robbins, or visit the grandparents, and take them back home and put them to bed.

QUESTION 29

Did you make any concerted effort to single kids out?

DOUG: We didn't really need to. We had three, and they were two years apart, and it was very easy for me to get to know them all well. I can easily see if we had seven or eight children, I would have an obligation to make a point of singling kids out, because you get to a certain number and somebody is going to get lost in the shuffle.

NANCY: Also, if I had to go somewhere, I might take one this time and another the next time. I just don't think it was organized. Since Doug and I both worked at Logos School, we were there with our children for everything.

DOUG: Also, when the kids got older, we wanted our kids to have the liberty to bring their friends over and to just show up. And that involves food and activities, not necessarily organized activities, but a safe place for the kids to come and hang out and just have it be a good place for doing that. We always made a point of not insisting that "You must stay home" or "It's gotta be here," but having it be the kind of place where the kids would want to have the fun be. Also, that made it easy for us to snoopervise.